AF575911

Major League SOCCER

Sporting Kansas City

Marylou Morano Kjelle

Mitchell Lane
PUBLISHERS

2001 SW 31st Avenue
Hallandale, FL 33009
www.mitchelllane.com

Printing 1 2 3 4 5 6 7 8

Designer: Ed Morgan
Editor: Sharon F. Doorasamy

Library of Congress Cataloging-in-Publication Data

Names: Kjelle, Marylou Morano, author.
Title: Sporting Kansas City / by Marylou Morano Kjelle.
Description: Hallandale, FL : Mitchell Lane Publishers, 2019. | Series: Major League Soccer | Includes bibliographical references and index.
Identifiers: LCCN 2018003133| ISBN 9781680202663 (library bound) | ISBN 9781680202670 (ebook)
Subjects: LCSH: Sporting Kansas City (Soccer team)—History—Juvenile literature.
Classification: LCC GV943.6.S667 K54 2018 | DDC 796.334/640977866—dc23
LC record available at https://lccn.loc.gov/2018003133

PHOTO CREDITS: Design Elements, freepik.com, Cover Photo: William Purnell/Icon Sportswire, p. 5 Scott Halleran/Getty Images, p. 6 freepik.com, p. 9 Scott Indermaur/MLS/Allsport Getty Images, p. 10 Rick Yeatt Getty Images, p. 12 Kyle Rivas/Getty Images, p. 15 freepik.com, p. 16 freepik.com, p. 17 freepik.com, p. 18 Bob Levey/Getty Images, p. 21 Andy Lyons /Allsport, p. 22 Robert Laberge /Allsport Getty Images, p. 25 freepik.com. p. 26-27 freepik.com

Contents

Words in **bold** throughout can be found in the Glossary.

A New League Forms

Each spring, North American soccer fans eagerly await the start of the Major League Soccer (MLS) season. The opening game in March kicks off many months of dribbling, shooting, passing, and scoring excitement. When the regular season ends in October, the team that has won the most games receives an award called the Supporters' Shield.

MLS enthusiasm doesn't stop at the end of the season. Postseason excitement continues with the MLS Cup Playoffs, where losing teams are eliminated from playing for the MLS Cup. The MLS Cup game is the **league's** playoff championship game. The team that wins the Cup will be the season's MLS Champion.

With all the fancy footwork that goes on during a soccer game, is it any wonder that soccer is the most popular sport in the world? More than 240 million people in more than 200 countries play soccer. In some places soccer is referred to as football. But in North America, football is a different sport altogether.

The Fédération Internationale de Football Association (FIFA) is an international organization based in Zurich, Switzerland. FIFA **oversees** the sport of soccer wherever it is played throughout the world. FIFA makes sure the rules of soccer are easy for players to understand. FIFA also sees to it that the game is played fairly. FIFA believes the power of soccer can be used to build a better future for all people, no matter where the game is played. One of the ways FIFA accomplishes its goals is by sponsoring challenging soccer tournaments. Two of FIFA's most well-known competitions are the World Cup and the Women's World Cup. These games are held in a different country every four years.

The Philip F. Anschutz Trophy is a silver trophy that is awarded to winners of the MLS Cup.

Chapter One

In the United States, soccer is managed by the United States Soccer Federation. This organization, which is also called U.S. Soccer, has been around for more than 100 years. U.S. Soccer controls the **amateur** and **professional** soccer games that are played by men, women, and youth in the United States. Members of U.S. National Soccer teams play in World Cup, Olympic, and **Paralympic** Games.

U.S. Soccer is a member of FIFA. In fact, it is because of FIFA that MLS was created. MLS is the professional league for men's soccer in the United States and Canada. In 1988, the United States placed a bid with FIFA to host the 1994 World Cup. Brazil and Morocco also wanted to hold the tournament, but the United States won the bid. From June 17, 1994, to July 17, 1994, the FIFA World Cup was held in nine U.S. cities. As part of the deal, however, U.S. Soccer had to promise to form a professional soccer league. MLS was officially created in February 1995.

The league started the 1996 season with 10 teams. Sports teams are also called **franchises** or clubs. Clubs are usually separated into conferences, which are groups of clubs that compete against one another. MLS is divided **geographically** into two conferences, an Eastern Conference and a Western Conference.

In a regular season, each team plays 34 games. Seventeen games are at home and 17 are played away. In the postseason, which starts in November, the six teams in each conference with the most points advance to the playoffs. These six teams play one another. Then the best team from each conference competes for the MLS Cup.

MLS has grown over the years. Today, 22 teams are members of MLS. Nineteen teams are from the United States, and three are from Canada. MLS hopes to have 24 clubs playing in its league by 2020.

Fun Facts

1. The nine U.S. cities in which the 1994 World Cup was played were Pasadena and Stanford, California; Pontiac, Michigan; Dallas, Texas; East Rutherford, New Jersey; Orlando, Florida; Foxborough, Massachusetts; Chicago, Illinois, and Washington, D.C. There were 52 games in the tournament and the total attendance at all games was a record-breaking 3.5 million fans.

2. The **inaugural** MLS game was held on April 6, 1996, between the San Jose Clash and D.C. United at Spartan Stadium in San Jose, California. The score was 1–0 in favor of D.C. United. Striker Eric Wynalda scored the first goal in MLS history.

3. The 10 teams that made up MLS's first season in 1996 were Columbus Crew, D.C. United, New England Revolution, NY/NJ MetroStars, Tampa Bay Mutiny, Colorado Rapids, Dallas Burn, Kansas City Wiz, Los Angeles Galaxy, and San Jose Clash.

A Team of Two Cities

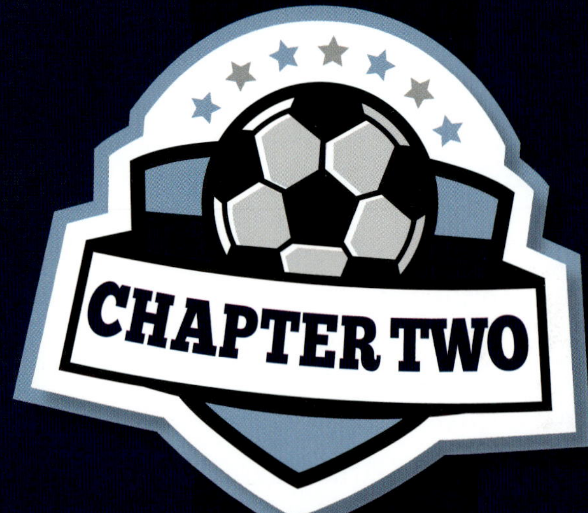

Sporting Kansas City was one of the first 10 teams to join the MLS when it was formed in 1995. At the time, Sporting Kansas City was known as the Kansas City Wiz. Fans often called the team the Wiz for short. The Wiz was founded and owned by businessman and sports promoter, Lamar Hunt. Ron Newman was the team's first head coach.

MLS first placed the Wiz, which was based in Kansas City, Missouri, into its Western Conference. Over the years, however, MLS has moved the team back and forth between the Eastern and Western conferences. Currently, Sporting Kansas City is in the Western Conference.

Preki of the Kansas City Wiz controls the ball during a 3-0 win over the Colorado Rapids at Arrowhead Stadium in Kansas City, Missouri, in April 1996.

The Wiz played their first game on April 13, 1996, at Arrowhead Stadium in Kansas City, Missouri. Thousands of Wiz fans were in the stadium cheering for the team as they competed against the Colorado Rapids. The Wiz won 3–0. This first win was just the start of a great first MLS season for the Wiz. The team placed fifth in the 1996 regular season, and their 17–15 record got them into the first ever MLS Playoffs. However, the Wiz lost the Western Conference Final to the LA Galaxy, 2–1 and finished third in the playoffs.

Chapter Two

Damian (*left*) of the Dallas Burn, Richard Gough (*center*) and goalkeeper Mike Amman of the Kansas City Wizards during the Cotton Bowl in Dallas, Texas, in June 1997

In the 1997 season, with a record of 21–11, the team, now called the Kansas City Wizards, again made it into the Western Conference Semifinals. But once more, their hopes for the MLS Cup were shattered. They were defeated in the first round of the playoffs by the Colorado Rapids, 3–0 . The next two years were not good for the Kansas City Wizards. They ended up in last place in the Western Conference in both years. But they didn't stay down for long. In 2000, the team won the MLS Cup in a match with Chicago Fire. The score was 1–0. The Wizards also won the Supporters' Shield that same year.

The Kansas City Wizards competed for the MLS Cup again in 2004 but lost to D.C. United, 3–2. They advanced to the MLS Cup Playoffs in 2013 and won the MLS Cup again that year by beating Real Salt Lake, 7–6.

The Kansas City Wizards went through a lot of changes over the years. When they won their second MLS Cup in 2013, the Kansas City Wizards were no longer owned by Lamar Hunt. The team wasn't even called the Kansas City Wizards. In 2006, Lamar Hunt had sold the Kansas City Wizards to a small group of Kansas City, Missouri, **entrepreneurs** who owned a business which is now called Sporting Club. The new owners saw that the team lacked an identity, and it had a small fan base.

Chapter Two

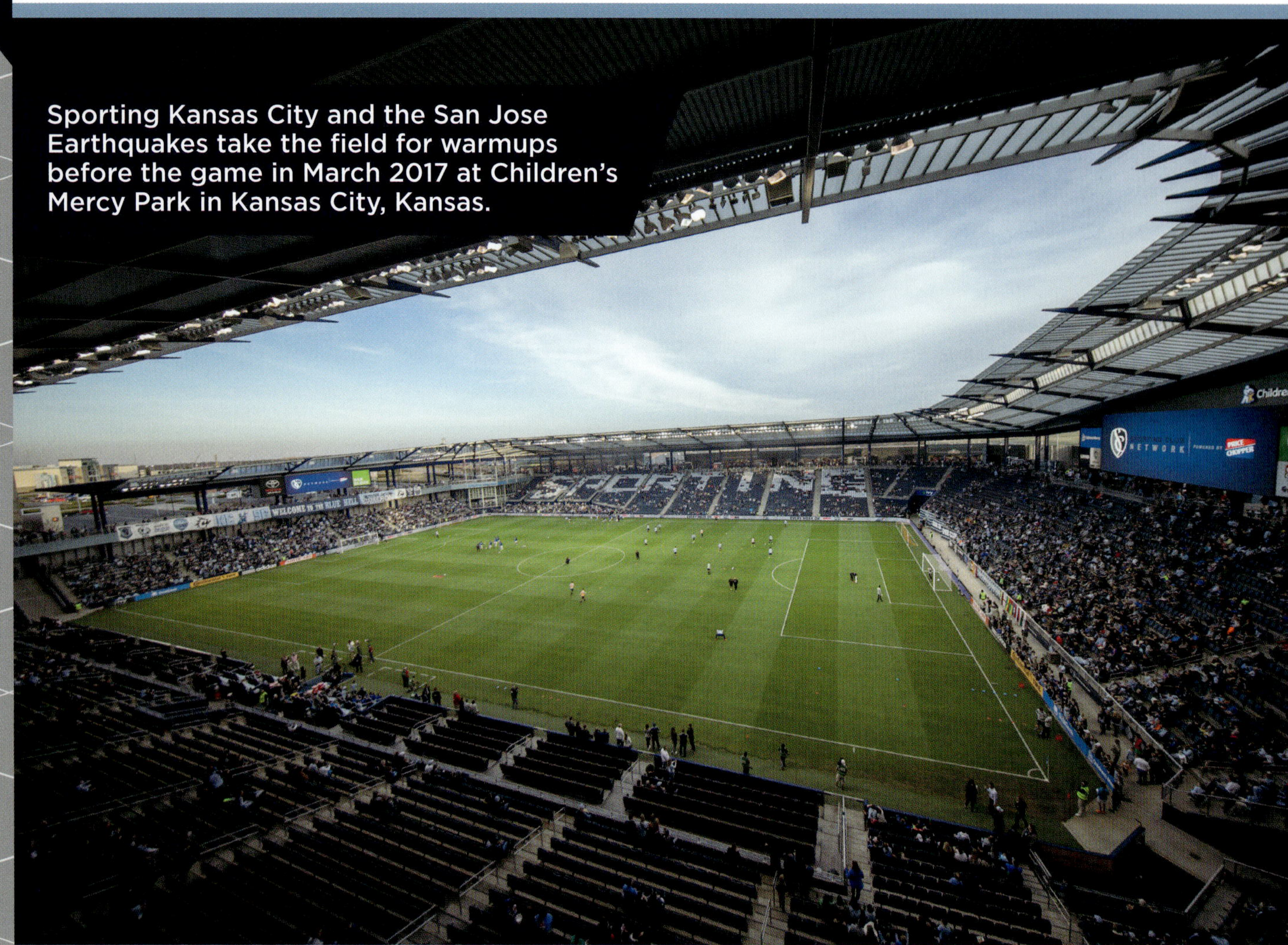

Sporting Kansas City and the San Jose Earthquakes take the field for warmups before the game in March 2017 at Children's Mercy Park in Kansas City, Kansas.

In 2011, Sporting Club made the first step in **rebranding** the club. It changed the team's name to Sporting Kansas City. The next year, Sporting Club opened a new soccer stadium in Kansas City, Kansas, called Children's Mercy Park. This is where Sporting Kansas City plays their home games. Being based in Kansas City, Missouri, and having a home stadium in Kansas City, Kansas, makes Sporting Kansas City unique among soccer clubs. You could say it is a team of two cities.

Both Sporting Kansas City and Sporting Club are involved in the community. They work with organizations such as the Make-a-Wish Foundation, a charity that grants wishes to sick children. Sporting Kansas City is also involved in developing new soccer talent. The team sponsors the Sporting Player Development Training System. This program offers young players extra soccer training for all levels of the game at Sporting Kansas City Academy.

Fun Facts

1. The players who made up the original Kansas City Wiz team came from the United States, Canada, Nigeria, England, Jamaica, Scotland, Cameroon, and Zimbabwe.

2. In addition to owning the Kansas City Wizards, Lamar Hunt also owned two other soccer teams, the Columbus Crew and the Dallas Burn (now known as FC Dallas), and one football team, the Kansas City Chiefs. Hunt was also a founder of the American Football League and a promoter of tennis and other sports. He is the first person to ever use the saying, "Super Bowl." In 1999, the U.S. Open Cup, an American soccer competition, was renamed the "Lamar Hunt U.S. Open Cup" in his honor. Lamar Hunt died in 2006 of cancer at the age of 74.

3. Some believed the name, the Wiz, came from *The Wizard of Oz*, which took place in Kansas. The electronic store, Nobody Beats the Wiz, said the soccer team was using its name illegally. Fans did not like the name either and asked the team to change it. After its first season, the Kansas City Wiz changed its name to the Kansas City Wizards.

The Pigskin Sport

No one knows exactly where or when soccer started, but the sport, or something close to it, goes way back in time. An early form of soccer, called *Ts'u Chu*, was played in ancient China more than 2000 years ago. Back then, players stuffed a ball made from animal hides with hair and feathers and kicked it through two posts. Early Greek, Roman, and Central American civilizations played a similar sport.

Native Americans used a stuffed deerskin to play *Pasuckquakkohowog*, which translates into "They gather to play ball with the foot." It is this early use of animal skins as a ball that gave soccer the nickname "pigskin sport." The Scotts wrote rules for soccer in the 1300s, but England brought soccer into the modern times. Many of the rules used by soccer players today were introduced in England more than 100 years ago.

So, what's so great about kicking a ball around a field? Just about everything! To start, soccer is one of just a handful of sports that can be played both inside on a court as well as outside on a field. The **objective** of soccer is to shoot the ball over the opposing team's goal line. The goal line is in the goal area, which is a rectangular area with a net located at each end of the playing area. This section of the field is also called the goalie box.

Chapter Three

Each team has its own goalie box and each team defends it with a special player called a goalkeeper, or keeper, for short. Goalkeepers are also called goalies. A goalie's job is to prevent a ball sent by the opposing, or competing, team from crossing the goal line. Each time a ball crosses the goal line, a goal is scored and one point is awarded to the team who sent it. Each team tries to score as many goals as possible, and the team that gets the most points wins the game. In addition to direct kicks, points can also be scored by penalty kicks and corner kicks.

Eleven players in total—the goalie and four defenders, four midfielders, and two strikers—play on the field. The goalie differs from the other players in two major ways. While the field players run up and down the field, goalies usually stay pretty close to the goal line. After all, it's difficult to defend an area if you aren't near it. In addition, a field player can use any part of his body except his hands, to propel a ball toward the opposing team's goal line. Goalies, on the other hand, may use their hands and arms, as well as any other part of their bodies, to stop the ball from crossing the goal line and prevent the other team from scoring.

Soccer games last 90 minutes, and they are divided into two 45-minute playing times. Each game begins with a kickoff. All field players except the goalie must be on their side of the halfway line (the line that divides the soccer field into two equal parts) as the first team kicks the ball toward the opposing team's goal area. Then it is the opposing team's turn to kick. Kickoffs also begin the second half of the game. If there is a tied score at the end of the game, one of two things may happen: the game goes into extra time or it is declared a draw.

Defenders usually play behind the halfway line. A defender looks for ways to intercept, or "steal," the ball to keep the opposing team from scoring. Midfielders are important to both the defense and **offense** of the team. They run, dribble, and pass the ball to other teammates as they move it toward the goal line. Forwards, also known as strikers, do most of the shooting.

All sports have a set of rules for players to follow, and soccer is no exception. For example, players are not allowed to **intentionally** push, shove, hit, trip, bump into, or touch another player in any other way. Players who do not conduct themselves in a sportsmanship-like manner are handed a yellow card, which is a warning. A player who commits a serious error, such as being disrespectful to another player or a referee, is given a red card. A player who receives a red card (or two yellow cards in the same game) must immediately leave the game.

Aurelien Collin (*center*) reacts after getting a yellow card against the Houston Dynamo in May 2013.

Soccer is demanding, yet fun, challenging, yet exciting, and strenuous, yet rewarding. It's no wonder soccer is the most popular sport in the world.

Fun Facts

1 Sporting Kansas City plays in American soccer competitions as well. The team has also won the U.S. Open Cup in 2004, 2012, and 2015.

2 One way soccer teams encourage the excitement and enthusiasm of their fans is with mascots. A mascot is a person or character that symbolizes the team. Mascots appear at all games. They sometimes appear at community events as well. Sporting Kansas City's official mascot is "Blue the Dog."

3 As with any sport, soccer has its own unique language and terms. Here are a few:

Assist—a pass that results in a goal

Corner Kick—a method of restarting play when the ball goes out of bounds and the ball is placed inside the corner arc at the nearest corner flagpost

Dribble—to keeping the ball in constant motion by carrying it with the foot

Penalty Kick—a free kick taken from the penalty spot with only the goalkeeper to beat

Pitch—the soccer field

Shoot—sending the ball, either by using the foot or the head, towards the goal

Shutout—when one team prevents the other from scoring a point. Also called a " clean sheet"

Twenty-two Seasons and Counting

A sports team is only as good as its players, and many players have contributed to the success of Sporting Kansas City over the years. You could say the midfielder, Mike Sorber, is the first player in Sporting Kansas City history because he was the first player signed to the Wiz in 1996. Sorber went on to play in 28 games and score four goals for Kansas City. He is now retired and works as an assistant coach for the Philadelphia Union.

Vitalis Takawira is a player from Zimbabwe who goes by the nickname "Digital." Digital was the first player to score for the Kansas City Wiz during their first game back on April 6, 1996. This makes him the first player to score a goal in Kansas City MLS history. Digital played the forward and midfielder positions.

He had a special move that isn't related to the game. He would get down on his hands and knees and do the "Digital Crawl" to celebrate scoring a goal.

Another Kansas City Wiz forward player, Frank Klopas, also scored a goal in the Wiz's first game. Klopas, who was born in Greece, left the Wiz after its 1997 season to play for Chicago Fire. He now works as a TV commentator.

The midfielder, Preki, whose full name is Predrag Radosavljević, was born in Serbia. He was also one of the original Kansas City Wiz members who played in the first game. Preki has won the MLS Most Valuable Player (MVP) award twice. This award is given each season to a player the MLS players, the MLS management, and the media feel is the most important to the League. Preki also played for the United States Men's Team at the 1998 FIFA World Cup. He was **inducted** into the American National Soccer Hall of Fame in 2010.

Preki of the USA dribbles the ball while the defenders try to take it from him during a game against Scotland at the RFK Stadium in Washington, D.C., 1998.

Chapter Four

Miklos Molnar of the Kansas City Wizards leaps for the ball during a game against the Los Angeles Galaxy at the Rose Bowl in Pasadena, California.

The Kansas City Wizards won their first MLS Cup in 2000. That season, one of the top goal scorers for the team was Miklos Molnar. Molnar was born in Denmark and had played professional football there before switching to soccer. During the 2000 season, Molnar scored 12 goals for the Wizards. That same season, Kansas City Wizards captain Tony Meola was named Goalkeeper of the Year, MLS's Most Valuable Player, and MLS Cup MVP. Meola has also played in two World Cups.

More recently, the defender Aurélien Collin, who was born in France, was selected as MVP in the 2013 MLS Cup championship. He left Sporting Kansas City and joined Orlando City Soccer Club in 2015. In 2017 he moved yet again, to the New York Red Bulls.

On July 1, 2015, during the Lamar Hunt U.S. Open Cup soccer match game against FC United, Sporting Kansas City forward Dom Dwyer became the first player in club history to score four times in one game. He also played for the U.S. Men's National team in the 2017 CONCACAF Gold Cup.

Whenever and wherever Sporting Kansas City plays, it's sure to be a sporting good game!

Fun Facts

1. **Over the years, Sporting Kansas City has played in three stadiums. The Wiz played in Arrowhead Stadium in Kansas City, Missouri, from 1996 to 2007. The Wizards played in Community America Ballpark in Kansas City, Kansas, from 2008–2010. Sporting Kansas City opened the 2011 season at Children's Mercy Park, in Kansas City, Kansas.**

2. **Soccer uniforms are also called kits. Sporting Kansas City's kits have changed over the years. Currently the uniform shirt is blue with a white collar. The gray, blue, and black Sporting Kansas City emblem is over the heart. The shorts are white and the socks are blue.**

3. **Sporting Kansas City started the 2016 soccer season as the U.S. Open Cup Champions. This made the team eligible to play in the 2016–17 CONCACAF Champions League for the third time. (They also played in 2000 and 2013.) CONCACAF stands for the Confederation of North, Central American and Caribbean Association Football. CONCACAF is part of FIFA.**

International MLS Spirit

MLS is a North American league, but almost half of its players were born in countries other than the United States and Canada. MLS players come from Argentina, England, and Ghana. Brazil, Jamaica, France, and Colombia also have many players. In 2017, players from 67 different countries were part of MLS. This makes MLS one of the most diverse leagues in North America.

Since the members of an international team speak many languages, it can be difficult for players to communicate on the soccer field. Luckily, most of the moves or plays that take place during a soccer game are **universal**. This means that they are the same throughout the world. Players are good at anticipating what their team members will do on the field. A soccer player doesn't always have to communicate by talking. He just has to work with his team members to make a goal and win the game.

Chapter Five

Still, there are times when a player and a coach have to say a few words to each other. Many players, but not all, learn English in their native countries. These players are usually able to communicate with the coaches and their teammates. Some coaches are **fluent** in several languages, and they can talk directly to their players. Other coaches use translators to help with communication. Often a team has more than one player from the same country. The players who speak English translate for the players who do not.

International players have to adjust to being a part of the MLS in other ways. Players from other countries must get used to living in a new country. Having loved ones nearby helps with the transition, so they bring their families along when they can. There's new food, **currency**, climates, living conditions, means of travel, and social rules to get used to. In addition, players must fly thousands of miles through different time zones to get to a game. So there is jet lag to deal with also.

It might take an international player a few MLS seasons to get used to all the changes that need to be made. Still, with time and patience, a player can learn to adjust to a new league, a new team, and a new country.

Fun Facts

1 Some current Sporting Kansas City players who were born outside the United States are: Dom Dwyer, *forward*, England; Latif Blessing, *forward*, Ghanna; Roger Espinoza, *forward*, Honduras; Jimmy Medranda, *midfielder*, Columbia; Soni Mustivar, *midfielder*, Haiti; Igor Juliao, *defender*, Brazil; and Daniel Salloi, *attacker*, Hungary.

2 Different countries have different names for soccer. The French call soccer football, for example. Italians say *calcio*, the Irish say *sacra*, and the Polish say *pitka noza*.

What You Should Know

- Sporting Kansas City has had three team names since starting in 1996.
- Sporting Kansas City has played in both the Eastern and Western conference for MLS.
- Sporting Kansas City won the MLS Cup and the Supporters' Shield in 2000.
- Sporting Kansas City won the MLS Cup again in 2013.
- Sporting Kansas City won the U.S. Open Cup in 2004, 2012, and 2015.
- Sporting Kansas City started Sporting Kansas Legends in 2013 to honor people who play a role in Sporting Kansas City organization.
- Sporting Kansas City sponsors Centers of Excellence where SKC coaches help boys 11 and younger improve their soccer

Quick Stats 2016-2017 Season

Performance Score: 5344

Total Goals Scored: 41

Goals Conceded: 38

Shot accuracy: 41 percent

Sporting Kansas City Timeline

1993	The formation of Major League Soccer is announced.
1994	The U.S. hosts the 1994 FIFA World Cup in nine American cities.
1995	The formation of the Kansas City Wiz is announced; the team becomes one of the first teams to join MLS; Mike Sorber becomes the first player in Kansas City Wiz history.
1996	The first MLS game is played on April 6 between the San Jose Clash and D.C. United. The Kansas City Wiz plays its first game at Arrowhead Stadium on April 13.
1997	The Kansas City Wiz's name is changed to Kansas City Wizards.
2000	The Kansas City Wizards win the MLS Cup, beating Chicago Fire 1-0 on October 15. The team also wins the Supporters' Shield.
2004	The Kansas City Wizards win the U.S. Open Cup, beating Chicago Fire 1-0 on October 22.
2006	Lamar Hunt sells the Kansas City Wizards to a group of Kansas City entrepreneurs.
2010	The Kansas City Wizards are rebranded as Sporting Kansas City.
2011	The first Sporting Kansas City game is played at Children's Mercy Park on June 9.
2012	Sporting Kansas City wins the U.S. Open Cup for the second time, beating the Seattle Sounders FC on August 8.
2013	Sporting Kansas City wins MLS Cup, beating Real Salt Lake 7-6 on December 7.
2015	Sporting Kansas City wins U.S. Open Cup for the third time, beating the Philadelphia Union on September 30.
2018	Sporting Kansas City opens the season playing host to the New York City FC on March 4.

Glossary

amateur
An athlete who is not paid for playing a sport

bid
To make an offer

currency
Money

diagonal
Extending from one edge to another

entrepreneur
A person who starts a new undertaking at great risk

fluent
Speaking or writing a language with ease

franchise
A professional sports team

geographical
Pertaining to a region

inaugural
Relating to a new beginning

induct
To bring in as a member

intentional
Something done on purpose

league
A group or organization of things that are the same

objective
A goal or purpose

offense
The players who try to stop the other team from scoring a goal

oversee
To manage or supervise

Paralympic
Games for people with disabilities

professional
Doing something that provides an income or a means of support

rebrand
To change the image of a company or sports team

universal
Something that can be applied in all cases

Further Reading

Downing, Erin. *For Soccer-Crazy Girls Only: Everything Great about Soccer*. New York: Feiwel & Friends, 2014.

Edwards, Larry. *The Best Soccer Players of All Time*. CreateSpace Independent Publishing Platform, 2015.

Jökulsson, Illugi. *Stars of World Soccer*. New York: Abbeyville Press, 2015.

Kansas City Star. *We Love Ya! Sporting Kansas City 2013 MLS Champions*. Kansas City: Kansas City Star Books, 2014.

Rausch, David. *Major League Soccer*. North Mankato, MN: Epic, 2014.

On the Internet

MLS Soccer Website
https://www.mlssoccer.com

Soccer Terms Glossary. SoccerAmerica
https://www.socceramerica.com/glossary/

Sporting Kansas City Website
https://www.sportingkc.com

Index

About the Author

Marylou Morano Kjelle is a college professor and freelance writer who has written dozens of nonfiction books for readers of all ages, including biographies of soccer players Josh Wolf and Tim Howard. She has never played soccer but she has spent many hours on the sidelines as a soccer mom.